IMAGES
of America

TIGARD

The Quello House shown is typical of Tigard's "Age of Elegance," and the area has always been refined and prosperous. The Quello House was previously known as the Shaver-Bilyeu House. This Late Victorian Queen Anne Cottage–style home was originally built by William and Lizzie Shaver in 1906 and purchased and improved by J.C. Bilyeu around 1935. Today, the home is owned by retired pastor Dan Quello and his wife, Jacque, who was Oregon's Mother of the Year in 2008. The Shaver-Bilyeu home was placed on the National Register of Historic Places in 1993. In 1995, Quello House won the National Trust's Great American Home Award. (Photograph by the author.)

ON THE COVER: Tigard residents wait for the train at the Oregon Electric (OE) Railway station about 1908, when it began operation. The OE contributed to Tigard's transformation from rural to urban community. (Courtesy Tigard Historical Association.)

IMAGES
of America

TIGARD

Barbara Bennett Peterson, PhD

ARCADIA
PUBLISHING

Published by Arcadia Publishing
Charleston, South Carolina

Library of Congress Control Number: 2012942742

For all general information, please contact Arcadia Publishing:
Telephone 843-853-2070
Fax 843-853-0044
E-mail sales@arcadiapublishing.com
For customer service and orders:
Toll-Free 1-888-313-2665

Visit us on the Internet at www.arcadiapublishing.com

*Celebrating the 50th anniversary
of the incorporation of the City of Tigard on September 11, 2011,
and to the citizens of Tigard*

CONTENTS

ACKNOWLEDGMENTS

Images of America: *Tigard* came to fruition because of numerous individuals dedicating their time and talents to this significant endeavor. Grateful appreciation is extended to Margaret Barnes, director of library services; Sean Garvey, adult services librarian; Joyce Niewendorp, adult services senior librarian affiliated with the Tigard Public Library; Mary and Don Feller, past presidents of the Tigard Historical Association; Martha Worley, current president of the THA; Curtis Tigard; Paul and Betty Clark; and members of the Board of Directors of the Tigard Historical Association: Valri Darling, John Frewing, Betty Parker, David and Sandra Tigard, Gary and Sue Lass, Karyn Smith, Leah McCann, Linda Gaarde Drake, Darin and Liz Christensen, Marian Schendel, Mary Ann Hulquist, Patricia and Oliver Keerins, Phil Pasteris, Sally Jones, Elaine Wallick, Ruth Croft, Karen Sadler-Fredd, Niranjan Ramakrishnan, and Yvonne Brod. These dedicated individuals carry on the local history and traditions of the pioneering Tigard family who gave their name to our community. Historical pictures for this book were, unless otherwise noted, provided by the Tigard Public Library's Local History Room and the Archives of the Tigard Historical Association. These images are considered to be in the public domain and have been used with permission.

Additional historical archives were tapped at the Broadway Rose Theatre Company, Tigard, Oregon, the Oregon Historical Society in Portland, Oregon, the US Forest Service, Cathlapotle, a Native American site in the Ridgefield Washington National Wildlife Refuge, North Central Washington Museum, and the National Archives Canada.

Thanks are also expressed to Tigard's mayor Craig Dirksen and all members of Tigard's city government and official departments and bureaus who gave of their expertise and assistance to this public history. September 11, 2011, marked the 50th anniversary of the incorporation of the city of Tigard on that date in 1961. A public celebration was held at the Tigard Public Library, headlined by notable family icon Curtis Tigard and Mayor Dirkson, who stressed the importance of remembering and celebrating our city's history.

In specific instances, private individuals have also contributed their family historical photographs, and their contributions are so noted in this book's appropriate captions. Donations of private photographs for this book's collection have come from Curtis Tigard and the Tigard family, including the family scrapbook belonging to Rosa Hohman Tigard, Valri Darling, Sandra Hanneman, and the Panck family; Estelle Gaarde Rasmussen and Richard Gaarde; Marion Hill; Cari Froeber and the Summerfield Civic Association; the Sturm family; the Frewing family; the Finley family; Barbara Bennett Peterson; Paul and Betty Clark; the Broadway Rose Theatre and photographer Craig Mitchelldyer; and the American Legion of Tigard. Their names appear following the captions.

—Barbara Bennett Peterson, PhD (Mrs. Frank L.)
Former Professor of American History
Oregon State University
Member Tigard Historical Association Board of Directors
Docent, Local History Room, Tigard Public Library

INTRODUCTION

Tigard, Oregon, in the Northern Willamette Valley, has a population of nearly 48,000 and is Oregon's 12th largest city, incorporated on September 11, 1961. The land area is approximately 10.9 square miles. Tigard is a suburb of Portland, Oregon, and is south of Portland and Beaverton, west of Lake Oswego, and north of Tualatin. Earliest recorded inhabitants were the Tualatin, Native Americans who were also known by their original tribal name, Atfalati Kalapuya. Native Americans burned the forests to clear the timber, create open prairies, and invigorate the soil for planting, lessons passed on to the settlers who came over the Oregon Trail as early as 1851 to settle in the valley and establish homesteads on donation land claims.

Solomon Richardson, his elder brother George Richardson, and Wilson Tigard were among the first pioneers. Their community was originally called East Butte, where George Richardson donated part of his claim to build a community school in a small log cabin. In 1896, a larger frame schoolhouse was constructed, and at the turn of the 20th century, the school added a second story. The community's name was changed to Tigardville when Charles Fremont Tigard, a son of Wilson and Mary Ann Yoes Tigard, opened a post office and a family general store in 1886. The store served the prosperous farmers of the Tigardville community as it expanded from timber and farming to a more widely diversified agricultural and residential area. John Gaarde opened a successful blacksmith shop across from the Tigard General Store, and for a time, this area of Pacific Highway served as the focal point of the community.

Emanuel Evangelical Church, the first community church, was built in 1886 at the base of Bull Mountain. The early 20th century heralded improvements to Tigard's Main Street with the arrival of Germania Hall and various small businesses. Boosterism for Tigardville became rampant, with land developers and promoters such as Edward Quackenbush subdividing farmlands and extolling the virtues of healthy, rural living. The town of Tigardville became known as Tigard in 1908 when the railroad came through, and local residents wanted to distinguish Tigard from Wilsonville, the next stop on the rail line. New businesses sprang up near the rail depot in Tigard's downtown. The telephone service began in 1908; the Oregon Electric Railway station opened in 1908 and began service to Tigard from Portland; and by 1911, electricity was extended to Tigard's farming community as part of the rural electrification process.

People from Portland began to settle in Tigard, commuting to work via rail. Subdivisions were laid out, and migrations from the city followed as services improved. Social and cultural events abounded, sponsored by the Tigard Grange, the Masonic Lodge, and various philanthropic clubs. Cars arrived in the 1920s, gradually replacing the horse and carriage. By the 1930s, streets were paved. New schools and churches blossomed. The Great Depression did not hurt as deeply in Tigard as the independent farmer was able to sustain a degree of self-sufficiency and also find outlets to sell his produce via rail transport to Portland's Yamhill Market. The 1940s saw young men join the armed services and serve honorably in military service at home and abroad. Prosperity boomed again in the 1950s, the population continued to move from Portland to the suburbs, and the City of Tigard was incorporated in 1961. The Tigard Area Chamber of Commerce took the lead in self-rule, and the measure supporting the city's incorporation was placed on the ballot as early as June 1958. Interstate 5 and Oregon Route 217 are major freeways to Tigard, and Oregon Route 99 West and Route 210 offer adjunct connecting links supplemented by TriMet rail service. Since the construction of these new transportation arteries in the 1950s and 1960s, ever-larger parcels of residential and business land have been annexed to Tigard as residents have requested affiliation with the city, enabling them to share the benefits of urban amenities and public services. King City and Summerfield, both adult living communities, increased the popularity of Tigard as a residential destination with health and leisure activities.

Today, pride in Tigard's pioneering past can be seen in the restored John Tigard House Museum, administered by the Tigard Historical Association. It is now in the National Register of Historic Places. The Pioneer Cemetery above Pacific Highway shelters deceased Tigard pioneers and their families; graves are often maintained by Tigard Rotary members. The Queen Anne–style Quello House is also a lovely reminder of Tigard's rural past. Today's Quello House was originally the Shaver House, built by William and Lizzie Shaver in 1906 on what had been a part of a donation land claim made in 1852 by William's father, Adam. Adam Shaver also gave the land on which the original Durham School was built. The Tigard Public Library now stands at the former location of the Grimstad Welcome Ranch, which once raised Shetland ponies. Cook Park represents the best in urban planning with its banks along the Tualatin River, boat access, and friendly, spacious grounds featuring the Butterfly Garden and walking paths. The annual Tigard Balloon Festival in June originated as part of the Portland Rose Festival and attracts thousands of visitors each year. The Tigard Family Festival annually celebrates the birth of Tigard as an independent city.

One

NATIVE AMERICANS AND EARLY PIONEERS

The Native Americans of the Tigard-Tualatin region were called the Atfalati Kalapuyas. The cedar plank house pictured above is similar to those built by the Atfalati Kalapuyas throughout the Willamette Valley. Cathlapotle was a large Native American (Chinook) village on the Columbia River in the Portland Basin to which the Native peoples of Tigard-Tualatin, the Atfalati Kalapuya, traveled to secure salmon and other articles of exchange. Cathlapotle was composed of 14 cedar plank houses and was visited by Meriwether Lewis, William Clark, and other members of the Corps of Discovery on November 5, 1805. Seven canoes came out to greet and trade with Lewis and Clark. Explorers estimated Cathlapotle's population to be around 900 Native Americans in 1805. Today, recreated early Cathlapotle is within the Ridgefield Washington National Wildlife Refuge.

Cathlapotle was strategically placed along the Columbia River midway between the coast and the interior. Each plank house had holes in the roof to vent smoke from their cook fires as shown in this photograph. The Atfalati from the Tigard-Tualatin region and the inhabitants of Cathlapotle relied upon *wapato*, a wetland tuber similar to potato as a basic food source, in addition to fish, berries, and plants.

The entry door was a low, round opening over which skins were hung to block the cold. The design on the outside had symbolic meaning and acted as a protective totem. The figure in this design is wearing a typical conical rain hat made from natural, woven fibers found in the wetlands adjacent to the plank house.

This is the interior of a typical Native American cedar plank house with double-decker sleeping bunks along the sides and the firebox cooking area in the center. The natural-colored ridgepole in the back with the face figure marks the chief's living quarters and his family's firebox.

A low fire was often kept smoldering for warmth, and Native Americans slept in bunks built along the walls facing the fire pit, where food was roasted, baked, or smoked. The dominant colors of the interior and other artifacts are red and black, signifying life and death.

The Atfalati burned some forestlands to clear areas for planting crops, but wood sources were carefully managed for cooking and heating. Game grazed on the cleared land. Stone tools were made by flaking obsidian or flint knapping. Wood was splintered using stone and bone tools like the ones pictured here.

Tule mats were made from bulrushes, which were gathered from the wetlands to be made into everything from sleeping mats, clothing, baskets, canoe ropes, drugs, food (pounded into flour to make bread), and summerhouse covers. This image shows cooking tongs on the tule mat and a wooden water bowl to put out the cooking fire.

Obsidian, granite, and antler bone used for making Native American tools are shown in their natural forms. Obsidian was traded over long distances with some varieties coming from the region of modern Bend, Oregon and from as far away as the Canadian Rockies. These items were also made into beads, ornaments, and jewelry and were used in trade and in ceremonies.

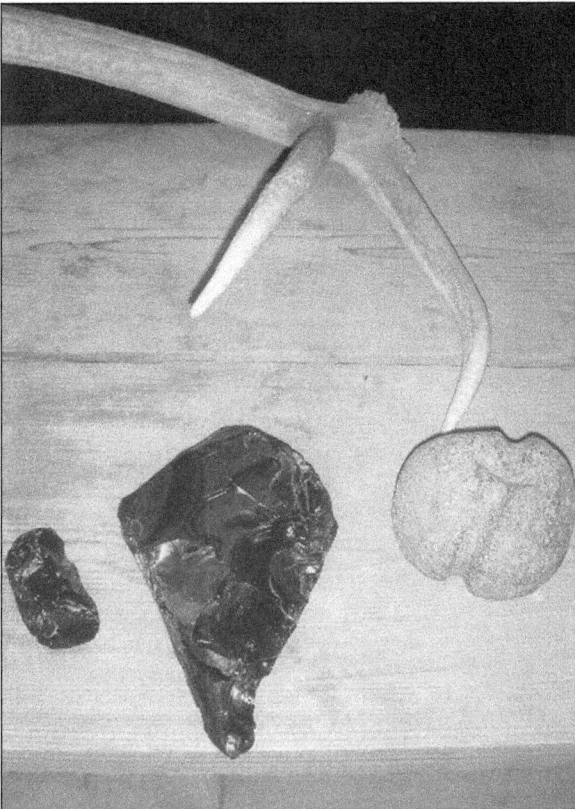

Native Americans of the Columbia and Willamette River Basin used the small basket for collecting berries, the mortar and pestle for grinding nuts and seeds, stone weights for fishing nets, a handheld bailing "cradle" to bail water from canoes, and gathered fibers to make into clothing. These items might also be exchanged at large summer meetings, where weddings, public ceremonies, or funerals took place.

13

Paul Kane (1810–1871), an Irish-born Canadian, traveled throughout the Willamette Valley in the 1840s painting Native Americans. His "Four Clackama Indians" (1848) is shown here. He also painted First Nations peoples in Canada on two visits in 1845 and from 1846 to 1848. On his second trip, he traveled from Toronto, Ontario, across the Rocky Mountains to Fort Vancouver, sketching the Native Americans of the Oregon Country.

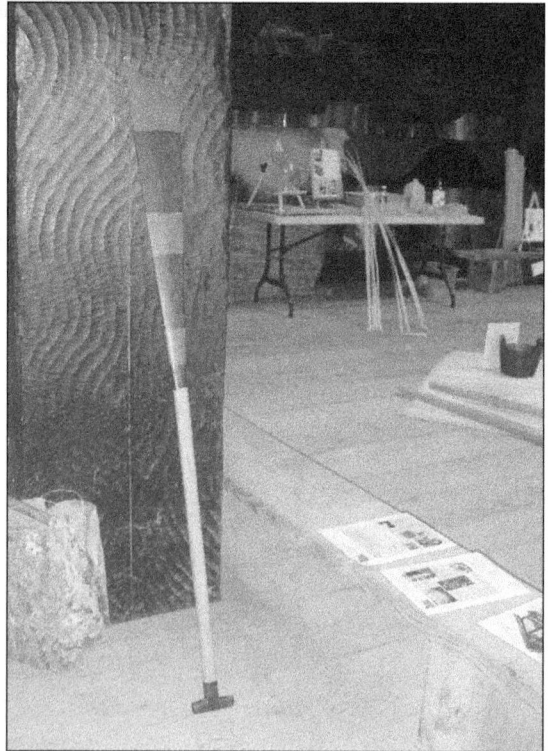

Canoe paddles were of a distinctive shape with the rounded center so as to be able to push the canoe off rounded rocks. The paddles were decorated with red and black as were their canoes. Native Americans such as the Atfalati Kalapuya of Tigard-Tualatin traveled long distances to fishing grounds along the Columbia River. Salmon were dried and smoked for winter use or exchanged in trade.

Summer tule mat teepees were easily taken down and moved as they traveled to new fishing or hunting grounds. Kinship, traced through the male line, was the basis of Kalapuyan society. In 1855, the US government concluded a treaty with the Willamette Valley tribes. The Kalapuyans were moved to the Grande Ronde Reservation in 1856. The Atfalati could also speak the Chinook jargon as a trading language.

The symbol of being born free was a flat head among the lower Columbia River Native Americans such as the Atfalati Kalapuya of Tigard-Tualatin and their neighbors, the Chinook. Slaves were not allowed to use the cradleboard, which flattened the frontal occipital portion of children's heads. On March 1, 1833, William Walker published a letter in an issue of New York's *Christian Advocate and Journal*, explaining the process.

Paul Kane became famous in Canada and America for his paintings of Native Americans, including many from the Tigard-Tualatin Valley. William Walker's original drawing in 1833 may have been an influence in Kane's paintings as he strove for accuracy, as in this image, "Caw Wacham," which shows the cradleboard. The strings are tightened to bring the leather flap down on the infant's head to flatten the skull—a sign of free status.

The earliest white settlers in the Pacific Northwest were fur trappers and traders. English artist Frances Anne Hopkins (1838–1919) captured the early life of the voyageurs in the Pacific Northwest in "Shooting the Rapids" (1879) as she and her husband, Edward Hopkins, an official for the Hudson Bay Company, traveled extensively by canoe along fur-trading routes.

An artist exploring the Columbia in 1841 on the Charles Wilkes Expedition drew Kalapuyan men, images that later appeared in Charles Pickering's *The Races of Men and Their Geographical Distribution* in 1848 and 1854. The Gibbs-Starling map of 1851 indicates an area of 12 square miles around Wapato Lake designated to the Atfalati. Wapato (potato-like) was an important food source for Native Americans, as was camas (onion-like).

The Oregon Trail started in Missouri and headed west to the Pacific. Most pioneers stopped at The Dalles, Oregon, and built flat boats on which to float down the Columbia River to Milwaukie and Oregon City, where they dispersed into farmlands of the future Tigard. Oxen-drawn covered wagons carried flour, bacon, rice, salt, coffee, tea, sugar, beans, vinegar, baking soda, corn meal, and dried fruit.

Families crossed the Great Plains together to make their home in Oregon. Children of the early frontier in the region that became Tigard, Oregon, helped civilize the landscape, calling forth the need for rural schools and churches. Note the girls' laced high-top shoes, appropriate for farmlands and muddy roads, and the leggings worn under their dresses.

Wilson McClendon (also Mcclendon) Tigard (born 1826) was patriarch of the Tigard family. With his wife, Mary Ann (Yoes), (born 1830), Tigard came across the Oregon Trail and settled in East Butte. The city became known as Tigardville when their son Charles Fremont Tigard ran a post office in his general store beginning in 1886, and the postal station address was renamed Tigardville. The city later became Tigard when the electric railway came through in 1908.

Mary Ann "Polly" (Yoes) Tigard journeyed to Oregon after crossing the Oregon Trail with her husband, Wilson Tigard, and their eldest son, John W. Tigard. The Tigards had 10 children: John W. (born 1850), Mary Ann (born 1852), Sarah Adeline (born 1854), Emaline (born 1856), Josephine Gertrude (born 1858), Francis (born 1860), Charles Fremont (born 1862), Abraham Lincoln (born 1864), Conrad S. (born 1866), and Hugh Butler (born 1868).

This article, from the inaugural issue of the *Tigard Sentinel*, on August 1, 1924, tells the story of the Tigard family. Pictured are founders Wilson and Mary Ann Tigard.

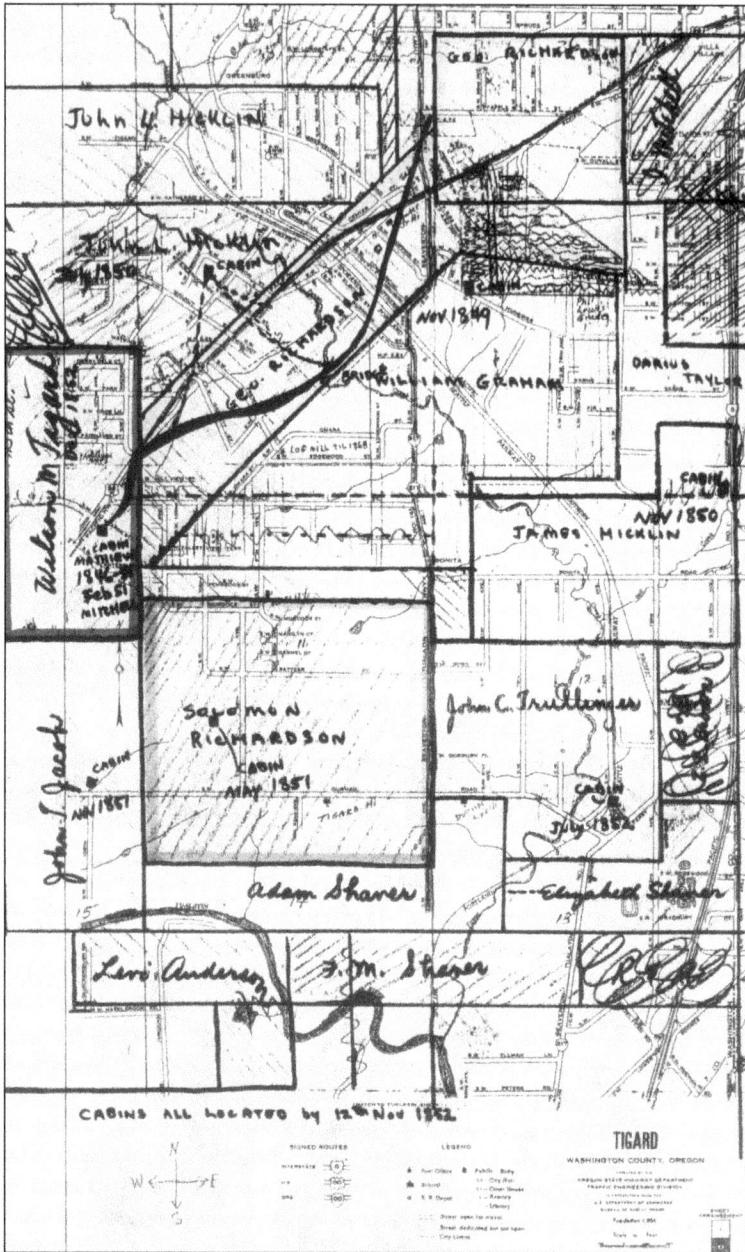

This map shows the early donation land claims of Wilson Tigard, George Richardson, and Solomon Richardson, all pioneers who came across the Oregon Trail between 1847 and 1852 with their families and filed claims for 320 acres of land that they would settle and improve. Wilson Tigard purchased a claim of 320 acres from a previous claimant, Mr. Matthews, and paid in kind with two Spanish cows he had received from a neighbor named George Richardson. The Richardsons convinced the Tigards to stay and build a school for local children. The cow debt was paid by Wilson Tigard by clearing land and burning out stumps for George Richardson. Oregon's local government had begun with a provisional government formed in 1843, the negotiation of the Oregon Treaty of 1846, and the establishment of a territorial government in 1849. Oregon was admitted into the Union on February 12, 1859.

Augustus Fanno, after whom Tigard's Fanno Creek is named, received a donation land claim in 1847. He had migrated to Missouri, where he married Martha Ferguson; they had a son named Eugene. They left Independence, Missouri, for Oregon in 1846, taking six months to reach the Columbia River. Martha died upon arrival and was buried in Linn City.

Augustus remarried Rebecca Jane Denney (1819–1909), daughter of Fielding and Jane (Hicklin) Denney in 1851. She was a teacher and came west in 1849. The Fannos cultivated onions (yellow danvers) and aided other immigrants to the region, including the Tigards, paying them for their labor in supplies.

Augustus Fanno worked with the local Atfalati Kalapuya Indians and fished for trout in the Creek, which was named for Fanno. Kalapuyans are a linguistic identification and occupied the valley between the Coast Range and the Cascades. This sketch of an Atfalati and his tule mat hut was drawn in 1841 by Alfred T. Agate, a member of an expedition on behalf of the US government that was led by Lt. Charles Wilkes.

The restored Augustus Fanno House is surrounded by a white picket fence today. It was originally built in 1859 and is now in the National Register of Historic Places. The former Fanno Farm is part of the Fanno Creek Recreation Project and is located off Hall Boulevard on Creekside Drive, just east of the Hall-Greenway intersection. (Courtesy Paul Clark.)

AND LUCY
ARR. 1851, S.C. 1851

THOMAS
AND

THOMAS H. AND BERILLA
DENNEY
ARR. 1849
S.C. 1850

ALLEN AVENUE

ROBERT W. DENNEY

MARY ANN

TUCKER

Denney Mill, 1860s

Denney? Home, 1850's

Whitford Station, 1908

AARON AND ALMI DENNEY

DENNEY ROAD

HENRY B. AND

Early Community Center, 1840's

McKay/Progress School, Dist. 18. Est. 1870-1888.

Garden Home School, Dist. 6T, 1911

AUGUSTUS AND
REBECCA
FANNO

Fanno Creek

JAMES McKAY
S.C. 1853

ELIZABETH
TUCKER

GARDEN HOME ROAD

WILLIAM AND SARAH
CLEMMENS

HALL BLVD.

ARRIVED 1846/47
SETTLED
CLAIM 1847

Indian Campsite, 1850's

Fanno Station

Fanno Farm, 1852

Early School, before 1887

ALLEN RICHARDSON

Ames Chapel, before 1859

OLESON ROAD

JOHN D. AND

Blacksmith 1860s

JAMES AND MARY ANN
DAVIES

TAYLORS FERRY ROAD

MARY ANN
RICHARDSON

Greenway School, 1980

WILLIAM J.
AND
EMALINE
ROBINSON

Crescent Grove Cemetary, 1857

Hiteon School, Dist. 108, 1911

SCHOLLS FERRY ROAD

DAVID C.
GRAHAM
S.C. 1850

THOMAS AND NANCY STO
ARR. 1851, S.C. 1852

THOMAS
AND
MARGARET
McKAY

JAMES R. BENNETT

GEORGE AND
MARTHA RICHARDSON

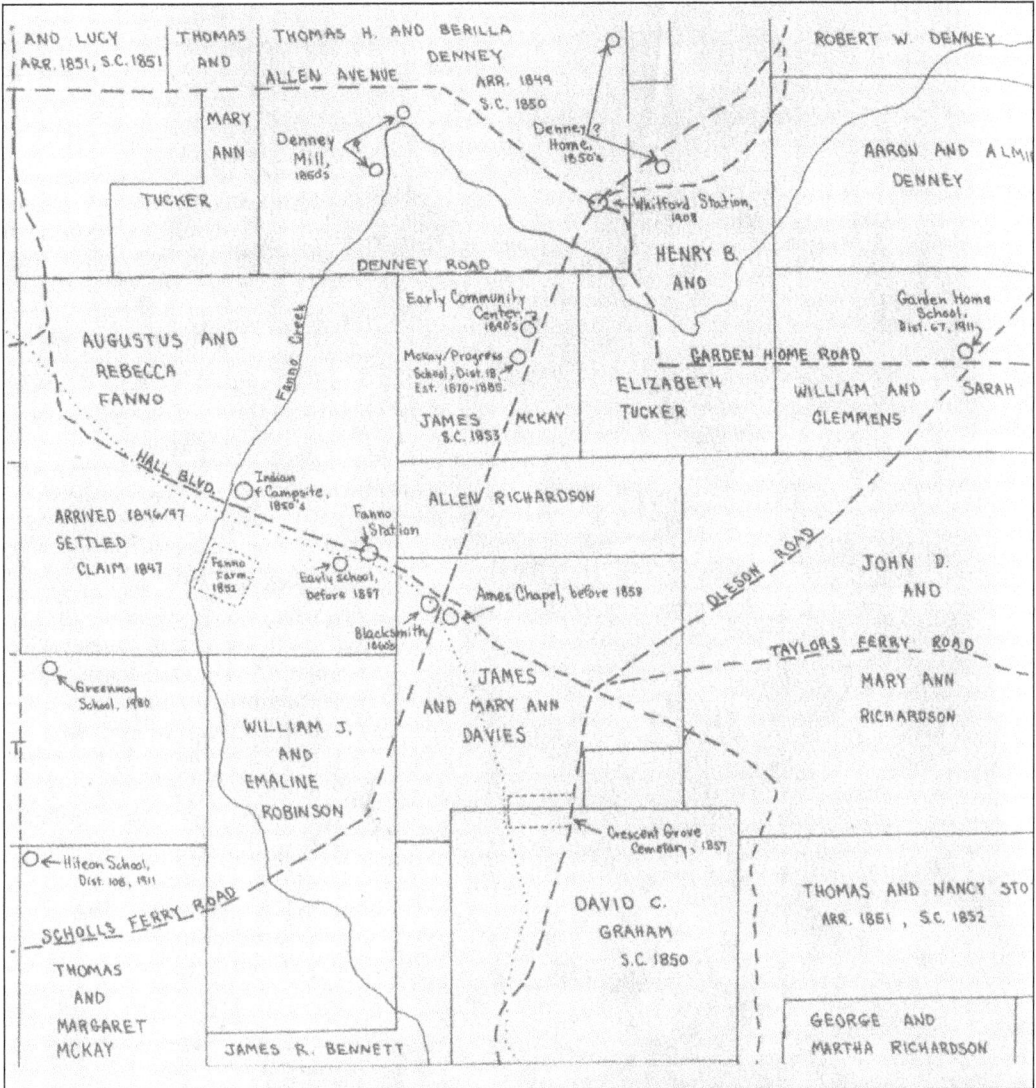

The original donation land claim (left center) of Augustus and Rebecca Fanno is shown on this map. Note in the lower right of this map the location of the donation land claim of George and Martha Richardson, who were also pillars of the community that became Tigard. George Richardson donated the land for the first East Butte School, a log cabin built in 1853. George's brother Solomon Richardson had the original donation land claim where Summerfield was later built in the mid-1970s.

Augustus Fanno was called the "Onion King" for the vast, rich farmlands where the Fannos raised onions, pictured here. He drained Beaverdam Lake, which covered nearly half of the future town site of Beaverton, and by draining swamps, lowland ponds, and lakes populated with beavers, Fanno was able to make the region a healthier place to reside with supplies of fresh water. (Courtesy Paul Clark)

Augustus Fanno expanded his land holdings and community influence. He was a deputy sheriff, teacher, and farmer, influential in developing Canyon Road between Beaverton and Portland, used to transport produce. He also donated the land on which Beaverton's first school district no. 48 was built. The original textbooks were ordered from missionaries in the Sandwich Islands (Hawaii). Beaverton's history was closely connected to that of Tigard's.

Two

EAST BUTTE BECOMES
A COMMUNITY

This c. 1895 image shows the children of Frank and Clara Fisher, pioneers in the area later known as Tigard. The children seated are, from left to right, Agnes, Ella, Genevieve, and Malinda. Son Edward Fisher is standing. The Fisher children attended East Butte School, which was the grade school serving the area in the 19th century. (Courtesy Valri Darling.)

The Fishers are another pioneer family that settled in East Butte, Tigard's original name. Frank Fisher was born May 16, 1857, in Marquette, Wisconsin, the son of German immigrants Carl and Augusta Fischer (later Fisher). Clara Hasse Fisher was born in Prussia on January 19, 1865, the daughter of Otto and Marie Hasse. She came to America with her parents when she was seven. Frank and Clara Fisher were early farmers in East Butte and are buried in the old Pioneer Cemetery on Little Bull Mountain above Pacific Highway. They had a baby daughter who died and was buried between them. The Fisher family includes, from left to right (front row) Genevieve, Clara (mother), Muriel; Frank (father), and Agnes; (second row) Ella, Edward, and Malinda. Edward Fisher and his wife, Rose, were buried in Crescent Grove Cemetery in Tigard. (Courtesy of Valri Darling.)

One of the earliest churches in the area that would become Tigard was the Emanuel Evangelical Church. The early services were in German. The church was erected in 1886 as the first permanent church in East Butte (later called Tigardville, then Tigard). The church stood at the base of Little Bull Mountain, and its Pioneer Cemetery is further up the hill. In 1919, the church was torn down when Pacific Highway was expanded. A new church was built about a mile north of the old church. In 1946, the Evangelical denomination merged with the United Brethren denomination and formed the Evangelical United Brethren Church (EUB). In 1968, a new denomination was formed called the Evangelical Church of North America. They built a new church on 121st Avenue called the Trinity Evangelical Church, which still owns the Pioneer Cemetery.

All members of the Evangelical Church, the first church in Tigard, are pictured here. Many are members of Tigard's first pioneering families who came to Oregon by traveling along the Oregon Trail in the 1850s and made donation land claims. The original Evangelical Church site was at the base of Little Bull Mountain, with its cemetery up the hill behind the church.

The earliest cemetery in the area belonging to the Emanuel Evangelical Church was known as the old Pioneer Cemetery and was located on Little Bull Mountain above Pacific Highway. Many of the early pioneers who made donation land claims are buried there. The cemetery remains today and is maintained by the Tigard Rotary.

Friedrick Johann Brandt was born in 1837 in Grabow, Mechlenburg-Schwern, Germany. He married Maria Schaffer in 1869 (died 1878). The couple had four children, all of whom died in a diphtheria epidemic in South Dakota. Friedrick remarried Maria Grabor, and they had four children: Sophia, Mary, Lydia, and John. This second family arrived in Tigardville in 1888 and farmed 20 acres across from the Odd Fellows Hall. Another daughter, Ella, was born here.

Maria Grabor Brandt is shown with her daughter, Ella Brandt, who is wearing a dress she made by hand. Maria's husband, Friedrick, assisted in the formation of the Evangelical Church, where German was used for the morning services and Sunday school, as so many of Tigardville's original settlers were German.

Gladys Beyer is a granddaughter of Friedrick and Maria Brandt and the daughter of Mary Brandt and her husband, Charles Beyer of Portland. The Beyers lived in Portland for a short time and then built a home on her parents' property at the corner of Pacific Highway and Watkins Street.

Durham, another community associated with Tigard, has existed since 1849. It was named for Albert Alonzo Durham, who was born in Genesee County, New York, and migrated to Oregon in 1847. He built several sawmills, including one in Oswego named for Oswego, New York, and in 1869, he built both a sawmill and a gristmill on Fanno Creek. The Durham schoolhouse, pictured here, was built in 1920.

Friedrich Sturm (1865–1945) and his wife, Gottliebin (1868–1903) Vogt Sturm, were married May 19, 1894, in Portland, Oregon. The Sturms settled on a farm in the area that became Tigard. Friedrich was born in Wurttemberg, Germany, and Gottliebin was born in Gutenberg, Germany. They had five children: Anna, Rudolph, Oscar, Gottlieb, and Christian. The Sturms are buried in the old Pioneer Cemetery on Little Bull Mountain, and their stone burial markers are written in German. (Courtesy Dale and Marilyn Sturm.)

Tigard was originally called Butte, or East Butte, and the original school was a log cabin constructed by the pioneers in 1853, replaced in 1869 with a frame building. Dating from 1896, this East Butte School was located where the Charles F. Tigard School is today. It included students from all elementary grades. Teachers boarded in private homes and were paid $20 per month.

The former one-story, frame East Butte School, built in 1896, became a two-story school about 1903, when the roof was literally raised. This six-room grade school was the early primary educational institution in the community that had started as East Butte, and the students read *McGuffey's Eclectic Reader and Spelling Book*. The school that became the Charles F. Tigard School was built on the site in 1922 and named for Charles F. Tigard in 1955.

East Butte School students are pictured from grades six, seven, eight, and nine, all in formal dress. The older students often helped the younger students with arithmetic and grammar. The school taught around 65 students annually.

East Butte essentially began as family farmland, and tremendous work was done to clear it, often through community efforts. Stumps were removed from the site with mule, horse, or oxen teams or were burned out.

The Hunziker Dairy near Garden Home is pictured in the late 1800s. Rudolph Hunziker, wearing a hat and coat in the center of the photograph, married Sophia Hoffman in 1894. They were both from Switzerland. They settled with their daughter Tillie on 115 acres of property purchased from the W.W. Graham donation land claim about 1896 and later, had a son, Edward. Rudolph Hunziker operated his dairy with his family on what became Hunziker Road.

Children learned to care for farm animals at an early age, which taught them to be self-sufficient and self-reliant. Education was important to the community, and many youth went to college and technical schools to learn engineering and agricultural skills necessary to farm development. This image shows Marian Biller Schendel with the family's grazing cows.

Constructing roads, surveying, building bridges, and raising barns were often communal tasks.

Gradually, frame homes were built and the farmlands prospered. Tigard became a region of fruit orchards, grain, onions, specialty nuts, flowers, livestock, and dairy cattle. This image shows an early home of Charles F. Tigard who became prominent in the community as farmer, merchant, postmaster, and legislator.

Homes became larger and grander as Tigard farmers were able to sell their produce in the growing metropolis of Portland, Oregon, accessed first by wagon and later, by rail. This home was originally built by Charlie Shamburg in the 1890s, and the family lived here until the 1920s when it became the Nash home. A number of Tigard's finest homes were Victorian Gothic and were surrounded by white picket fences.

Horse-drawn wagons were used to transport produce to larger markets. Later, transportation improved with the coming of the Oregon Electric in 1908. Canyon Road and Taylor's Ferry Road were major connections to Portland.

After prosperity came to Tigard, weddings became more elaborate. The carriage in this photograph was borrowed from the Portland Hotel for the wedding of Mary Brandt and Charles Beyer. Here it is in 1907 in front of the Brandt home on Pacific Highway.

Groundwater resources were tapped by windmills, and nearly every farm in Tigard had its own well. Pioneers also had access to the Tualatin River or Fanno Creek. This Tigard Historic Windmill is located on Southwest 121st Avenue. It was built in 1866 on the donation land claim of pioneer Edward Wood. Civic-minded volunteers, known as the Friends of the Windmill, restored it in 1983. It has since become a Tigard landmark.

This windmill supplied water for the crops of John Brandt and his wife, Helen Rehberg Brandt (married in 1907). Many of the larger farms in the Tigard-Tualatin area were family compounds wherein a number of generations lived and worked. Family farms were often subdivided among the children who wanted to continue to live in the area. John Brandt built this home in 1907 across the road from his parents.

Timber was an early industry in the Willamette Valley in addition to agriculture. As the Tualatin River flowed into the Willamette River, timber from the Tigard-Tualatin region was cut and made into lumber at the large mill at Oregon City. There was a ready market for local timber with the construction of new homes, businesses, fencing, and storage facilities, such as barns.

Covered bridges, such as Taylor's Ferry Bridge, were built to cross the Tualatin River. Many of these bridges remained tourist attractions, while the river still affords public recreation. The bridge had laminated wood floors with asphaltic wearing surfaces. The windows allowed light to enter the bridge for safety. This covered bridge was originally built for $12,968.

The early Butte Grange, local no. 148, affiliated with the National Grange of the Order of the Patrons of Husbandry (The Grange), was a strong political force in the community. The Grange was a national organization founded in 1874 to represent the interests of farmers and encouraged education, extension services, rural free delivery, and the farm credit service. The Grange exerted considerable political influence. Wilson Tigard donated an acre in 1875 on which Butte Grange was built.

The Butte Grange was organized in the home of W.W. Graham in April 1874. The first official meeting was May 6, 1874, with H.S. Stott, first steward of the Grange, and dedicated April 21, 1877. The Grange changed its name from Butte to Tigard on October 28, 1946. The Grange hosted dances, musicals, quilting bees, and rallies favorable to farming interests. The original Grange building was incorporated into a new structure built on Pacific Highway in 1926.

Pictured here are members of the Grebe family. From left to right are (first row) Henry (father), Florence, Evelyn, Arthur, Mildred, and Matilda (mother); (second row) Hulda, Walter, and Leoda.

Matilda (left) stands on the Grebe family porch with her mother, Fredericka Baatz. Children often took care of their parents on a family farm.

Typical transportation before the Oregon Electric and the automobile was the horse and buggy, driven in this image by Katie Voegelein. From left to right, Leoda Grebe, Katie Voegelein, Sam Voight, and Ella Brandt are riding with her from the Grebe farm on Taylor's Ferry Road.

Katherine "Katie" Voegelein is shown on the day of her eighth-grade graduation. The white graduation dresses often became summer wedding dresses. Education was very important to young women and men in Tigard's community, and many went on to obtain college degrees, especially in the sciences and medicine.

Leoda and Hulda Grebe grew up in Tigardville. Children in the Tigard region grew up working on their family farms, and their contributions were considerable. Family members sat for their formal portraits from a very young age, as life was precious, and prosperous farmers had the resources to document their lives.

St. Anthony's Catholic Church began as the Mission Church on Gaarde Road where St. Anthony's Cemetery is located. A priest would come from Oregon City for the services. This church was an early city focal point for both worship and philanthropy. Further amenities abounded in Tigard as farmers' prosperity spawned additional elegant churches and community-based social and cultural organizations. Churches acted as both youth and adult centers.

Mary Brandt was the sister of Ella Brandt, Fred Schamburg, and Sophia Schamburg. The Schamburg family lived near the Tualatin River. They built the Schamburg Bridge. The Gottlieb Schamburg family owned farm property on both sides of the river and built a hand-operated ferry to cross the river, which they later replaced with a bridge.

The Elsner family purchased the Schamburg place. Fritz Elsner, pictured here, was on the board of the First Bank of Tigard, organized by William Evans. This bank was owned locally by farmers and businessmen. Besides Elsner, the First Bank of Tigard board included Charles F. Tigard, G.A. Plieth, Pete Olson, Chris Christensen, and Herb McDonald. In 1940, the First Bank of Tigard was sold to US National Bank and became Tigard branch bank.

George Frewing and Mary Sumpton Frewing are pictured with their five children in 1896. From left to right are (first row) George, Mary, and Ada; (second row) Arthur, Harry, Mabel, and Bertram. George was from Cookham, Berkshire, England, and Mary was from Heston, Middlesex, England, and they settled in Tigardville in 1879. The elder Frewings purchased 115 acres of land (known as Frewing's Orchard Tract) on today's Frewing Street.

Harry Frewing, son of George and Mary Frewing, is pictured here as a young man. He worked throughout Southern Oregon on railroad construction and had a farm on Bull Mountain Road in Tigard where he raised Hereford cattle. People would give directions by saying, "Go past Harry Frewing's bulls up on the mountain." Frewing married Marie Jones from Roseburg, and they had two children: Leslie and Dorotha.

Arthur Frewing married Olive Wilson and had four children. Two of their children are pictured here: Raymond and Blanche; their other children were Eunice and Lucille. Arthur and Olive immigrated to Alberta Province, Canada. Raymond, his wife, Vernita, and their family later moved back to Hillsboro, Oregon, and their son Raymond Jr. moved to Aloha.

Bertram Frewing married Florence Koerner of Beef Bend Road. They developed an orchard after purchasing part of the land that belonged to his father, George Frewing. Bert and Florence had three children: Mabel, Edna, and Darrol. Florence's sister, Emma Koerner Behnke, is pictured above. The sisters' maternal grandfather, Gottlieb Schamburg, farmed on both sides of the Tualatin River and built a covered bridge known as the Schamburg Bridge.

Harvey Behnke (1896–1973) was the son of Emma Koerner and William F. Behnke (1872–1956). Harvey and his wife, Myrtle, had four children: Grace, Melvin, Dan, and Harvey Jr. Families in Tigard intermarried, thus preserving their land holdings and business interests for heirs.

Mrs. Foster is pictured here about 1906. She taught many children of East Butte and, later, Tigardville, and was respected and admired in the community.

Three

TIGARDVILLE AND THE AGE OF RURAL ELEGANCE

Commercial businesses sprang up to serve the needs of farmers. Charles F. Tigard's general store on pacific highway and Gaarde Street was a successful enterprise and housed Tigard's first post office in 1886. Charles F. Tigard used "Tigardville" as the mailing station address in honor of his parents, Wilson and Mary Ann Tigard, and the city's name became Tigardville about 1886. The name was later shortened to "Tigard" around 1908 after the Oregon Electric Railway had come through, and residents wanted to distinguish the Tigard station from the Wilsonville station.

Charles F. and Rosa Hohman Tigard stand at the entrance of their general merchandise store with their daughter Grace Tigard at the turn of the 20th century. Their private home, attached to the store, is on the left. The sign for the Tigardville post office can be seen on the building's front. In addition to running their store, the Tigards farmed 15 acres of fruits and berries. Charles F. Tigard was a merchant postmaster and first elected to the Oregon State Legislature in 1885. He registered voters and offered his store as a polling place.

Charles and Rosa Tigard are pictured here with their children Grace (in front of her mother), George, and Curtis (in the white christening suit). This frame home, facing Pacific Highway, was a fine, two-story Victorian residence typical of Tigard at the turn of the 20th century. Later, the structure was moved a block west and repositioned to face Gaarde Street.

Charles F. Tigard was president of the First Bank of Tigard from 1919 to 1942. This bank was owned by local farmers and businessmen. Charles Tigard also became a notary in 1924 and handled important business transactions such as writing wills and recording deeds for clients within his bank. Local banks had become an economic necessity as farmers prospered and as land and equipment sales increased. He attended the East Butte School in 1858 in its first log cabin and married Rosa Hohman in 1893. He was a member of Oregon's house of representatives in 1895 and 1911.

Charles F. Tigard is pictured as a young man. Charles' first wife was Anna Marion Greene; they were married in 1883 and divorced in 1885. They had a son, William W. Tigard, who drowned at age 20 in Canada.

Rosa Hohman, Charles F. Tigard's second wife, is seated in the left front row in this image showing the surviving children of Johanna Schneider Hohman Pollard taken after the death of William Pollard Sr. in 1893. From left to right are (first row) Rosa, William Henry Pollard, Johanna Pollard, and John Hohman; (second row) Nellie Pollard Godwin Price, Martha "Mattie" Webb MacDaniel, Anna Pollard McDonald, and Elizabeth Hohman Grove Vincent.

Conrad S. Tigard, the brother of John and Charles F. Tigard, is pictured here as a young man. A doctor of chiropractic medicine, he married Gussie Hahnen and had two children: Veda and Blanche.

John W. Tigard and his wife are pictured in front of their home on Pacific Highway. John logged with oxen and lived most of his life on his father's farm. He had a horse-drawn coach route into Portland from Tigard, making a roundtrip on Tuesdays and Fridays for 50¢. He was a member of the Odd Fellows Lodge and the Tigard Grange. He was killed in April 1931 as he crossed Pacific Highway to the Odd Fellows Lodge.

John Tigard's first wife was Emma Ornduff; they had two sons: Frank and Jessie. After her death, he married Sophia Schmidler, pictured above, who later burned to death in their home in January 1917 when her clothes caught fire. After Sophia's death, John Tigard married Ervilla Shaw, who had a daughter, Edith Adelaide, from a previous marriage. John and his brother Charles owned 20 acres of their parents' land.

The Victorian John Tigard House, constructed in 1880 by Wilson Tigard, was a wedding gift for his son John. The Tigard Historical Association was incorporated in 1978 to restore the John Tigard House and to preserve the cultural and historical legacy of the Tigard area. Now the John Tigard House Museum, this house was placed in the National Register of Historic Places on July 20, 1979. (Courtesy M.O. Stevens.)

John W. Tigard, the first son of Wilson and Mary Ann Tigard, is pictured here about the time the house was constructed in 1880. John lived in this house until his death in 1931. Like his father and mother, John Tigard was a pillar of the community, an enterprising farmer, and businessman.

East Butte School is pictured here about 1907. It burned down in 1918. Education was very important in the growing farming community, and educational contests were encouraged such as spelling bees, for which prizes were given. Many community children went on to college,

especially to the land grant institution known as Oregon Agricultural College, now Oregon State University, in Corvallis, Oregon.

Anna Pollard, half-sister of Rosa Hohman Tigard, is pictured on her graduation day, carrying a scrolled diploma. Anna's father, William H. Pollard Sr., bought 100 acres of farmland next to the Wilson Tigard farm. He married Johanna Schneider Hohman in 1876 in Cincinnati, Ohio. William Pollard Sr. was the father of Anna, Nellie, Mattie, and W.H. Pollard and was the stepfather of Rosa, Elizabeth, and John Hohman.

Anna Pollard McDonald is pictured after her marriage to Herb McDonald in 1910, when she ran the successful McDonald general store. The turn of the century in Tigard was a prosperous time; farmers could afford to buy both necessities and luxuries from the McDonald store.

Mattie Pollard, sister of Anna Pollard and half-sister to Rosa Hohman Tigard, is pictured as a young girl. She was one of Tigard's fashionable young ladies.

Mattie Pollard is shown as a young lady in the "Age of Elegance" in rural Tigard.

Dr. W.H. Pollard, the son of W.H. Pollard Sr. and brother of Anna Pollard, grew up on the family farm, went to medical school, and opened his first practice in Marcola and later, Springfield. He married Gustina Randell of Oregon City. His sister, Nellie Pollard, who had been widowed, also came to live in Marcola. With her second husband, Walter Price, she ran the local mercantile store.

John Hohman, brother to Rosa Hohman Tigard and half-brother to W.H. Pollard, was a teacher at the Bend School and a mentor to Tigard's children. The Pollards and the Hohmans remained close throughout their lives and were very active leaders in the Tigard community.

Hugh Butler Tigard (1868–1950), Wilson and Mary Ann Tigard's youngest son, opened a general store on Main Street in Tigard after the arrival of the Oregon Electric. Hugh Butler Tigard married Mamie "Daisy" Ledgerwood Landes, a widow with a daughter, Vivian (Mrs. Frank North). Butler was a member of the Odd Fellows Lodge and his wife was a member of the Rebekahs, female members of the lodge.

Hugh Butler Tigard's merchandise store, built 1911 on the corner of Tigard Avenue and Main Street, was typical of the new businesses that sprang up in response to the traffic generated by the rail depot. There were vast rows of candy to entice the children, and he filled their candy bags to the very top for 5¢.

Hugh Butler Tigard's stepdaughter Vivian is pictured in her white graduation dress. A collection of vintage dresses can be found in the John Tigard House Museum. Tigard women dressed elegantly for Grange parties, church, and charity events.

The Walter and Edah Upshaw family purchased Seven Gables on 100th Street in Tigard in 1909, planted 10 different varieties of apple trees, and raised poultry for Portland stores. Walter Upshaw was the Lion's Club's first president and was elevated to district governor in 1939. In 1924, he became Washington County horticulture inspector; by 1933, he had risen to become head of Portland's department of agriculture. Today, this is the Upshaw-Fredd home.

The family of Bartholomew Scheckla (1847–1930) and Tekla Koenig Scheckla (1850–1931) appears in this portrait from about 1900. From left to right are (first row) Mamie, Bartholomew, Frank, Tekla, Fred, and Rose; (second row) Gustav, Annie, Joseph, John, and Albert. They came to Tigard in 1881; in 1894, they purchased 40 acres of Solomon Richardson's donation land claim on Durham Road near Hall Boulevard to farm.

Boxing was viewed as a manly sport in the late 19th century. Theodore Roosevelt had been a boxer for his health, and many young men practiced the sport locally and nationally. In Tigard, the Scheckla boys practiced boxing, and their rounds were timed. Young men learned to defend themselves in preparation for real-life situations. Sometimes, competitive fights were held with prize money offered.

The first Tigard school bus, pictured here, transported children to and from Tigard grade school. Previously, schoolchildren rode their ponies to school and tethered them behind the schoolhouse.

Hannah Wood Christensen is pictured here. Her father, Edward Wood, was born in Canada in 1837. He had moved to Iowa at the age of 10 and later married Ann Margaret Grabel. The Woods came to Oregon in 1866. They settled and farmed a Donation Land Claim at the corner of Walnut and 121st Streets. Their daughter Hannah remained on the family farm and cared for her father and her husband, Chris Christensen.

This Spousta home, located on Bull Mountain on Beef Bend Road, is a reminder of the rural elegance of early Tigard. Their dairy farm delivered milk to households in large milk cans, carried first by a flatbed wagon, later, by truck.

Bend School was originally located on Beef Bend Road and educated the children from surrounding farms. Today, Bend School is a private residence at 147th Avenue and Beef Bend Road. A one-room school with eight rows of desks and eight grades, it averaged between 30 and 40 students per year. Reading, writing, arithmetic, penmanship, geography, health, social studies, and Oregon history were taught.

Charles "Bud" Beyer (1913–1992), the son of Mary Brandt and Charles Beyer, is going to Tigard grade school with his lunch pail. He represents Tigard's third generation. Many children grew up on Tigard's farms and remained to work the land with their parents, ultimately sharing in the family estate.

William "Willie" Tigard played on the Tigardville Baseball Team. Recreational teams like this one reflected Tigard's growing prosperity; players had more leisure time after the introduction of new technologies to farmlands.

The Tigardville Baseball Team was comprised of local players who played for fun and exercise against neighboring cities. Baseball had become a national leisure sport, and the team built local pride and community spirit. Baseball players were the heroes of Tigardville, and later, of the city of Tigard. The Tualatin Valley League, which consisted of Tigard, Beaverton, Hillsboro, Verboort, and Forest Grove, competed for the annual championship trophy.

Dr. Sylvester R. Vincent (seated), Art Vincent, Mrs. Vincent, and George Vincent are pictured standing in front of their home in Tigard. Dr. Sylvester Ruel Vincent graduated from Chicago's Hering Medical College in 1897 and became an expert in phrenology. He had married Tillie Preston in 1895, and they had two sons: George Sylvester (born 1896) and Arthur Herbert (born 1897). Tillie died in 1899. Soon after, Doctor Vincent came to live in Tigardville and opened a practice in Tualatin.

In 1904, the widowed Doctor Vincent married Elizabeth Hohman Grove, pictured above, a childless widow and sister of Rosa Hohman Tigard. Doctor Vincent brought the first automobile to Tigard, which was a 1911 Maxwell. His car was hit by a train at Tigard's Main Street crossing, and he died later from injuries sustained in 1918. His brother, Dr. Arthur Vincent, moved to Oregon and took over his brother's medical practice in Tualatin.

Four

TIGARD EQUALS OPPORTUNITY

Olga (Biller) Hoffman is pictured here on the docks at Konnigsberg, Germany. She and her brothers sold farm produce on the docks, carrying it from their home in Inse, Germany. Many immigrants from Germany and Northern Europe sought their fortunes in the Tigard region, as Oregon resembled their European homeland.

Hans and Ane Pederson, Danish immigrants, are buried in Tigard, Oregon. Their daughter Matilda Rasmine Pederson, born in Bernstofminde, Denmark, in 1873, married Jorgen "John" Nissen Gaarde. East Butte was a cosmopolitan blend of numerous European nationalities and several languages, which developed community spirit and fostered prosperity.

Pictured here are Matilda and Jorgen "John" Nissen Gaarde. John was born in 1864 in Gabel, Schleswig-Holstein, Germany, originally a part of Denmark. He served in the German army as a youth and was trained as a paramedic. Upon leaving the service, he was apprenticed to a blacksmith. Later, he opened a blacksmith shop in Garden Home in the early 1890s.

John Gaarde and Matilda (Pederson) were married in 1893. They came to Tigard and purchased a blacksmith shop from Mr. Cooperstein. The couple had four children: Anna (born 1894) (married William Heilman), Elizabeth (born 1899), Hans (born 1901 and married to Hilma Lien), and Marvin (born 1907 and married Ethel Hughes). Son Hans Gaarde is pictured at the side of the doorway of the family home.

John Gaarde is on horseback in front of the blacksmith's shop. His son Hans Gaarde is dressed in black next to the horse and rider.

John Gaarde's blacksmith shop gradually developed into an auto body and paint shop at the same location. John Gaarde rigged up this saw that is powered by a car. Estelle and Richard Gaarde, his grandchildren, are sitting in front.

John Gaarde repaired equipment essential to a farmer's livelihood, including wagon wheels, buggies, harvesters, threshers, and combines, plows, and tools of all types. He eventually diversified into automobile repair. He is pictured here with a blowtorch in hand. Blacksmiths, so important to their communities, were immortalized by Longfellow's poem "The Village Blacksmith."

Halvor and Gerstru Lien are pictured at their wedding. Marriages often blended farming families and their properties. (Courtesy Estelle Gaarde Rasmussen.)

Hilma Lien Gaarde (born 1901), daughter of Halvor and Gerstru Lien, was the wife of Hans Gaarde. Hans worked at a dairy in Tigard and was, like his father, a community leader. Hilma attended Tualatin High School and then Washington High School in Portland.

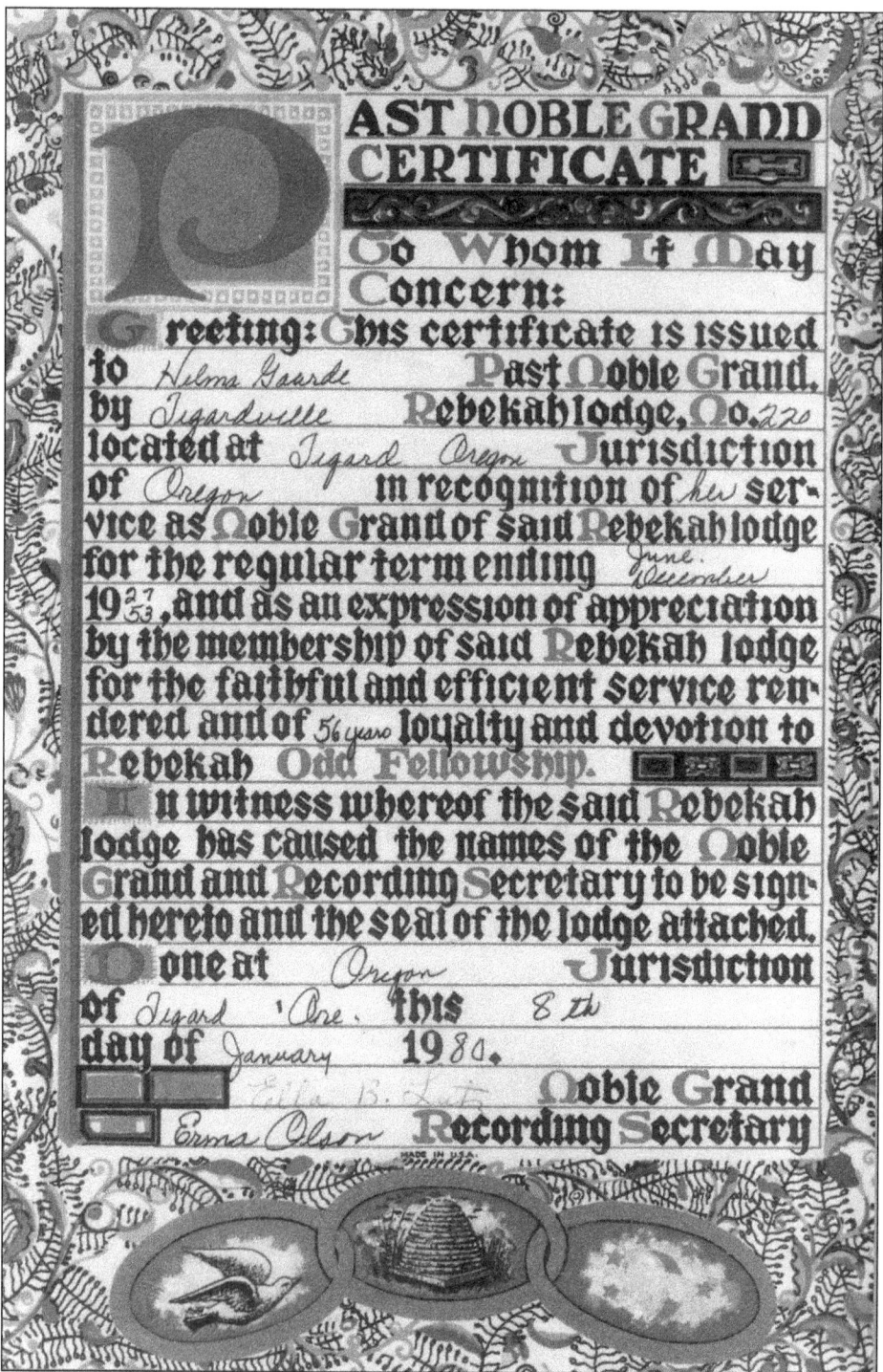

PAST NOBLE GRAND CERTIFICATE

To Whom It May Concern:

Greeting: This certificate is issued to *Hilma Gaarde* Past Noble Grand, by *Tigardville* Rebekah lodge, No. *220* located at *Tigard Oregon* Jurisdiction of *Oregon* in recognition of *her* service as Noble Grand of said Rebekah lodge for the regular term ending *June. December* 19*27 53*, and as an expression of appreciation by the membership of said Rebekah lodge for the faithful and efficient service rendered and of *56 years* loyalty and devotion to Rebekah Odd Fellowship. In witness whereof the said Rebekah lodge has caused the names of the Noble Grand and Recording Secretary to be signed hereto and the seal of the lodge attached. Done at *Oregon* Jurisdiction of *Tigard 'Ore.* this *8th* day of *January* 19*80.*

Tilla B. Lutz Noble Grand
Erma Olson Recording Secretary

Hilma Lien Gaarde was a member of Eastern Star and was a vocalist at weddings and funerals. During World War II, she served as a lookout for enemy planes on Little Bull Mountain. She was also a member of the Rebekah Lodge No. 220 in Tigard, as indicated by her award plaque that was presented to her in 1980 for serving as a "Noble Grand."

Hans Gaarde worked in his father's blacksmith shop and, later, the family automotive shop. In 1920, he went to work at the Red Rock Dairy, which was purchased by the Kraft Cheese Company in 1927. He married Hilma Lien in 1922, and they had two children: Richard John and Estelle. He also served on the Tigard School Board from 1936 to 1942.

Hans Gaarde worked at the Red Rock Dairy until 1941, when he went to work in the Oregon shipyards for four years during World War II. After the war, he worked for Del Monte Meat Company until 1963, when he retired. His wife, Hilma, is pictured with their son Richard John about 1927.

The Hasuike family of Tigard is pictured here in 1911. From left to right are (first row) Misao, Mankichi and Omitsu (second row) Ryozo, Shinzo, Torazo, and Isamu. Shinzo Hasuike had emigrated Hiroshima, Japan, to Tigardville in 1898, followed by his brothers Torazo and Ryozo. Together, the brothers purchased 40 acres on either side of Beef Bend Road, where they specialized in berries of all kinds and potatoes. In 1909, Torazo married Misao, and, following a flu epidemic in 1918, during which his two brothers Shinzo and Ryozo died, together they ran the farm with Isamu. Shinzo's widow, Omitsu, returned to Japan with their two daughters. Isamu eventually moved to Los Angeles and married Hisako from Hiroshima. Torazo and Misao Hasuike had eight children: Eichi (died as an infant in Japan), Josiko "Josi," Yoshio "Yosh," Tomo (Mrs. Sunamoto), Jim, Masoko, Shigeko, and Toshi "Tosh." In the 1950s, the Sunamoto family bought a farm in Tigard at 135th and Walnut Streets. The Hasuike brothers' parents Mankichi and Fusa Hasuike remained in Japan and did not immigrate to America with their sons, although their father, Mankichi, visited.

Claude and Alice Scoffins appear in this wedding photograph taken by Christopher Aerne and Carl Nordstrom, owner of a photography studio in Portland from 1899 to 1902. The Scoffins owned the property from Taylor's Ferry Road to Scoffins Street.

Germania Hall was the first building on Main Street in downtown Tigard about 1908. This hotel was built by the Adolph and Anna Schamoni family and was just south of the rail tracks on Main Street. Adolph Schamoni (1861–1936) was born in Germany, as was his wife, Anna Bungers Schamoni (1868–1927). Germania Hall featured a grocery and restaurant on the lower floor; a dance hall and hotel rooms were on the second floor.

The Schamoni family also built a livery stable at Main and Burnham Streets to accommodate their visitors and local residents. It was later purchased by the Kuehne family who loved horses. A young Harry Kuehne is pictured on horseback facing north on Main Street in Tigard. St. Anthony's Church is in the background.

The Kuehne Livery Stable later became a garage that repaired early motor vehicles and farm equipment. Harry Kuehne is pictured in front of his garage. Local farmers supported local businesses, and the community continued to grow prosperous through the partnership between farmers and merchants; eventually, a local bank was established to protect local interests and to serve community needs.

"Small Farms Pay" was a booklet written by Edward Quackenbush, a land promoter who bought farms and subdivided them to sell in smaller parcels. He came to Portland, Oregon, in 1865 and moved his family to the region that became Tigard in 1884. He sold land along the Tualatin River near where he lived in the early 1900s. He was a member of the Tigard Chamber of Commerce.

Martin Frank Bishop came to Tigard in 1908 from Hood River with his wife, Vina (Carnes) Bishop. He had read Quackenbush's publicity, bought property, and settled on eight acres of the former Willowbrook Farm in Tigard. Frank sold his produce in Portland at the Yamhill Market, as shown in this c. 1922 image, and used the Oregon Electric Railway to move his produce to market.

In 1901, the telephone was introduced to Tigardville. This image shows the inside of the Tigard Telephone Office where operator Rose Scheckla worked with the early switchboard. The telephone was an asset for business and health. One of the first uses for the phone was to call the doctor when a woman was about to give birth.

Rose Scheckla was Tigard's telephone operator in 1908 and 1909. Her parents, Bartholomew and Tekla Scheckla, were born in Prussia, immigrated to America, and arrived ultimately in Tigardville in 1894. Rose's father bought part of Solomon Richardson's original land claim, and her parents built a home near where Tigard High School is located today.

Gertrude and Elmer Thomas and their daughter Helen are pictured on the porch of the first telephone office in Tigard. The family lived here, and Gertrude cared for the telephone switchboard for 23 years (1910–1933). In 1911, Tigard was also connected to electricity and the telegraph. Gertrude became assistant postmaster from 1933 to 1953.

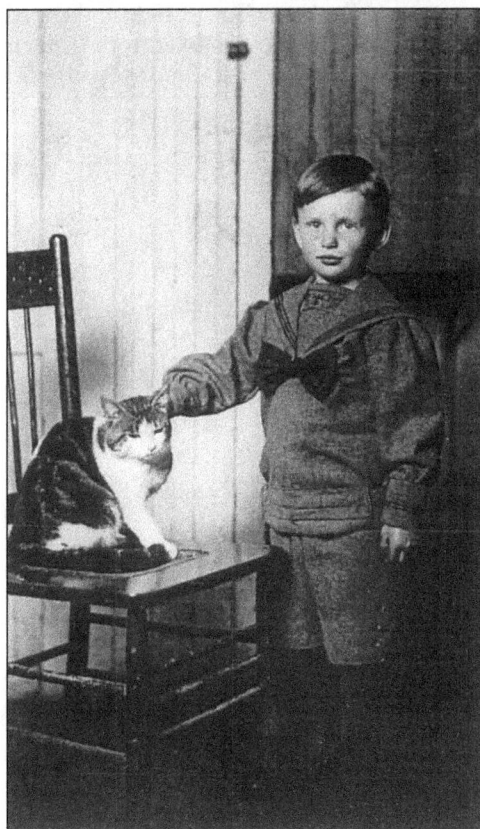

The son of Gertrude and Elmer Thomas, Leonard Thomas is pictured at the Tigard telephone office, where his family lived and safeguarded the switchboard. In 1901, the first local telephone was connected to the Tigardville store, owned by Charles F. Tigard.

Other improvements beyond the telephone included the Oregon Electric Railway, which started service on New Year's Day in 1908 and ended service in 1933. The OE was used to transport fresh fruits and vegetables to market in the growing metropolis of Portland. Fresh produce stimulated specialty restaurants, and Oregon has traditionally been known for its healthy, "green" living.

Local residents often rode the Oregon Electric into Portland for sightseeing, cultural events, or to work in the metropolis.

Oregon Electric Trece Station is pictured in 1926 with Grace Finley and her son Edward, age 14. It was located on present-day Hall Boulevard.

During World War I, young women from Tigard volunteered for the Nursing Corps in large numbers to aid the Allied effort in Europe. Here, two young women are graduating from Nursing School. Both young men and women from Tigard served abroad in European Theaters during the Great War (1914–1918).

The O'Mara family home, pictured here, belonged to Loyola and Mary Shipman O'Mara. Loyola O'Mara worked as a bookkeeper-accountant for Pacific Telephone and Telegraph; he became Washington County Road supervisor in 1922 and was later promoted to superintendent. Omara Street in Tigard commemorates his family.

Farmlands surrounding Bull Mountain were some of the richest in the valley. Better roads and improved technology facilitated community integration of rural and urban areas.

During the 1920s and 1930s, the Baggenstos family members were some of the most successful farmers in Tigard. Joseph Herman Baggenstos and his wife, Anna Marie Muller, were born in Gersau, Switzerland. Around 1920, they immigrated to Tigard, where they ran a dairy farm. During World War II, Joseph Baggenstos looked after the farm of the Hasuike family, which spoke of the integrity of Tigard's farming community.

The Joy Theater, Tigard's main cinema, was built on Pacific Highway in 1939. It offered family entertainment during the late Depression and remains today as an important landmark. Movies began in the 1920s with the silent "flickers." During World War II, the theater helped in the war bond drive, offering free admission to those who purchased a bond, and raised $5,175 in one evening. Seating is for 500 people, and J.W. DeYoung was the theater's architect.

Five

TIGARD BECOMES URBAN

The meat market on Main Street in downtown Tigard is pictured about 1919. Tigard's roads would soon be paved and curbs and parking established. In spite of the modernization that soon would come, a windmill can still be seen over the top of the building on the right. Groundwater wells and windmills would be utilized until the advent of public utilities in the 1930s.

During the 1920s and 1930s, garages sprang up to service automobiles. Establishments that had earlier repaired farming tools and vehicles, such as tractors or wagons, were converted to service cars. Tigard's prosperous residents purchased the newest technological inventions, including automobiles, and they often vacationed on the coast's beaches or ventured to Sucker Lake, now Lake Oswego.

John Jacob Panck (1886–1948) came to Tigard in 1918 and opened a poultry business. He was born in Germany and married Anna Catherine Eichhorn, born in Schleswig-Holstein, Germany, in 1890. John and Anna Panck are pictured with their daughters, from left to right, Eleanor, Florence (on lap), and Elizabeth. The original Panck farm was on the corner of McDonald and Omara Streets. (Courtesy Sandra Hanneman.)

By 1927, the Panck family's chicken business was thriving in Tigard. The image shows the Panck Hatchery, located on Pacific Highway, in the late 1920s. The hatchery was an important transition business between farm-raised poultry and the highly mechanized business it would become to serve a growing population.

Red and leghorn chickens were raised at the Panck hatchery. The increasing urbanization of Tigard provided an ever-increasing market for local poultry as the non-farming population grew. Competition lessened as many farms were sold for housing developments and the Pancks mechanized their operation to increase market share. Refrigeration allowed poultry to be shipped over ever-greater distances and to wider markets.

Richard and Estelle Gaarde, pictured about 1929, grew up in Tigard. Their grandfather John Gaarde had been Tigard's blacksmith. The Gaarde family, like the Tigard family, remained prominent members of Tigard's community. Gaarde Street bears their family name.

Hans and Hilma Gaarde and their children Richard and Estelle are shown about 1932.

Estelle Gaarde, the daughter of Hans and Hilma Gaarde, is pictured in the eighth grade at Charles F. Tigard Elementary School. The Gaarde family lived in Tigard for several generations.

CERTIFICATE OF PROMOTION

This will certify that _Estelle_

has satisfactorily completed the studies required by the State Course of Study in the

First Grade

School Dist. No. _23_ of Washington County Oregon, and is hereby promoted to the

Second Grade

Dated this _18_ day of _May_ 19_34_

Virginia E. Parks Teacher

Parents are urged to consult with teachers about the progress, deportment, etc., of their children.

Signature of Parent or Guardian

First Month

Second Month

Third Month _Hans Gaarde_

Fourth Month _Hans Gaarde_

Fifth Month

Sixth Month _Hans Gaarde_

Seventh Month _Mrs. Hans Gaarde_

Eighth Month

Ninth Month

Estelle Gaarde's May 1934 promotion certificate from the first grade is shown with the signature of her father, Hans Gaarde. She married Paul Rasmussen and had two children: Jan (Bain) and Tom.

The Schubring Biederman Store was located on Tigard's Main Street from 1925 to 1950. Across the street from the grocery, the store sold animal feed and garden supplies. August "Gus" Schubring started the store, and Wilbur Biederman bought into the store in 1925; it became known as the Schubring Biederman store over the next 25 years. Biederman is shown behind the counter, and Schubring stands with his daughter Betty and aunt Louise.

Wilbur Biederman supervised the feed store, and August Schubring administered the grocery store in their economic partnership. Ladies are pictured on the porch of the Schubring Biederman Store. Main Street was yet unpaved, but electricity had been introduced, something August Schubring was instrumental in securing for Tigard.

This late 1940s photograph of the Schubring store shows, from left to right, Tigard businesspeople Fred Hambach, George Brelin, Mrs. Hambach, Alexandarine Rankin, Marie Hoefs, Pauline Miller, and August Schubring.

The First Bank of Tigard became a branch of US National Bank, as pictured here. Curtis Tigard worked for US National Bank as its branch bank manager. The First Bank of Tigard was the first to have an electric sign, replaced by a neon sign in 1929. In 1938, a vault was added, and in 1939, 160 safety deposit boxes were installed. Residents could pay their taxes at the bank instead of driving to Hillsboro. The brick bank was constructed by H.F. Bonesteel.

Tigard resident Marion Hill's Combat Intelligence Section of the 365th Fighter Group, 9th Air Force, offered essential intelligence-gathering services that assisted in Allied Victory in Europe on May 8, 1945, V-E Day. Marion Hill is pictured in the center of the back row, the fourth from the left. He was part of the military buildup in England that led to the June 6, 1944, D-Day invasion. His combat unit went into France on June 16, 1944.

Combat Intelligence Section of 365th Fighter Group, 9th Air Force, is pictured during World War II in Chievres, Belgium, in October 1944. Tigard resident Marion Hill is in the middle row on the far right. His unit gathered information on enemy operations and positions throughout the war, especially during the Battle of the Bulge, when Germany attacked France, attempting to push back the Allied forces that had landed at Normandy.

Tigard citizen and resident of Summerfield, an active adult community, Marion Hill was awarded the Purple Heart after he was wounded during a German air raid on the French airfield at Metz, France, on January 1, 1945, during the Battle of the Bulge. This photograph shows his promotion to staff sergeant; later he was promoted to technical sergeant.

Marion and Susan Hill are shown after Marion returned home from the hospital. He went on to a successful 10-year career with the US Naval Ordnance Laboratory, where he discovered the compound TATB in 1952. Later, in 1960, he joined the Stanford Research Institute, where he founded their chemistry laboratory and served as its director for 17 years.

Richard Gaarde served in the Navy during World War II on USS LST-218. His ship saw action in the Gilbert, Marshall, and Mariana Islands, and he was involved with the capture of Saipan and Tinian. He returned from the war to become an electrician in Tigard, married Dorothy Huntsinger, and had three children: Richard, Linda (Drake), and Karin. (Courtesy Richard Gaarde.)

Carl Finley, pictured here about 1943, was the son of E.E. Finley, a longtime Tigard resident and community leader. Carl served in the Navy during World War II from 1942 to 1945 on the USS *Cascade* (AD–16), a destroyer tender, as a welder-diver. He earned $10 per hour and saved his wages to buy a home in Tigard after the war. Expanding as an urban area, Tigard offered jobs and security to veterans at war's end. (Courtesy Carl Finley.)

Jesse and Shirley Snyder are pictured in 1944. Jesse worked in the Swan Island Shipyard before joining the US Marine Corps, and Shirley worked in the shipyard's "mold loft." Using an awl, templates were created by scratching through the lines of the blueprint. From these templates, the steel was shaped in the plate shop. There were three eight-hour shifts, seven days a week. Shirley earned 90¢ an hour and worked in the mold loft for nearly two years.

The Kaiser Shipyards in Portland, Oregon, attracted hundreds of workers from Tigard-Tualatin areas. Here, the nightshift is arriving at Kaiser Shipyards during World War II. Shipyard workers built 435 ships including Liberty and Victory ships, military tankers, and aircraft carriers. Henry J. Kaiser had a government contract to construct these ships on Swan Island in Portland, and on May 19, 1941, his Oregon Shipbuilding Corporation launched the first Liberty ship, *The Star of Oregon*.

The Kaiser Shipyards

Monday, July 25
7–8 p.m. | Houghton Room

10,000 SHIPYARD WORKERS WANTED

Travel back in time and learn about the history and legacy of the Kaiser Shipyards, where over 700 vessels were constructed during World War II.

FOR VICTORY BUY UNITED STATES WAR BONDS AND STAMPS

The Ships We Build...

KAISER COMPANY, INC.

TIGARD PUBLIC LIBRARY
Serving the public since 1963
13500 SW Hall Blvd., Tigard, OR 97223 • 503-684-6537 • www.tigard-or.gov/library

Over 10,000 workers were recruited to work at Kaiser Shipyards. This poster from the Tigard Public Library advertises a free public presentation on the history of Portland's shipyards and their wartime achievements. War efforts on the home front were very important to military successes overseas.

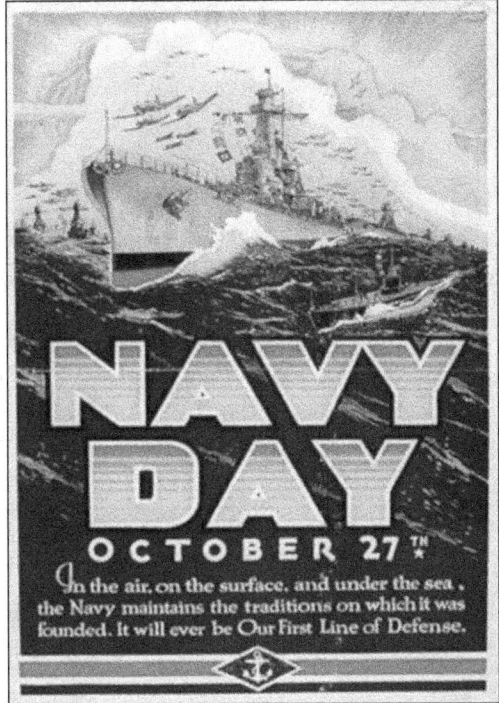

Morale posters were displayed throughout Tigard during World War II to rally citizens to the war effort. Posters reminded residents of sacrifices made from Pearl Harbor through the invasion of North Africa and the occupation of Tunisia before the campaign into Sicily and Italy and the 1944 invasion of Normandy on D-Day.

During World War II and through the 1950s, floating docks along the Tualatin River were created for visitors and the local community by motel/hotel parks, such as Roamer's Rest. These parks were the center of the recreational scene for local school-age youth, as well. The fresh water was clean and free of any debris, and these facilities were prime attractions in Tigard.

Grace Tigard Houghton (1901–1998), daughter of Charles Fremont and Rosa Tigard and sister to George (married Dorothy Dick) and Curtis Tigard, rides her bicycle in this post–World War II photograph.

Grace Tigard attended Lincoln High School before Tigard had a senior high. She also attended the University of Oregon, taught swimming at the YWCA in Boise, Idaho, and later, at the YWCA in San Francisco. She then attended Wellesley College for graduate studies. She taught at Pomona College in Claremont, California, and then returned to teach at Wellesley. (Courtesy Curtis Tigard.)

Curtis Tigard, son of Charles F. and Rosa Tigard, celebrated his 100th birthday on April 13, 2009. As a young man, he delivered the *Oregon Journal* and enjoyed catching moles, which were a problem for farmers. He went to Oregon Agricultural College (now OSU) and received a degree in banking and finance. Curtis worked for US Bank and served as manager of the Tigard branch until 1971. He and his first wife, Berniece Daniels Tigard, had a son named David.

Yearning to return to the West Coast, Grace Tigard accepted a teaching position in a high school in Piedmont, California, where she married Paul Houghton (1881–1942) in 1932. She is shown here in her wedding portrait. They lived in Claremont until the department of agriculture sent Paul to Pullman, Washington, and later Portland, Oregon, to work with the migratory labor camps. The Houghtons were asked to come to Washington, DC, and, later, Florida.

Grace Tigard Houghton returned to Tigard to assist her mother, Rosa Tigard, with whom she is shown. She taught at Twality Junior High School and then Reed College. She was a Mazama and climbed Mount Hood. She also enjoyed all-summer European bicycle trips. She donated funds to establish the Grace Tigard Houghton Room in the new Tigard Public Library, which displays her memorabilia.

Six

TIGARD TODAY

The Tigard Public Library is located at 13500 Southwest Hall Boulevard in Tigard, Oregon, today. This facility is a community resource with its public services, which includes a Local History Room, housing historical books, photographs, and newspapers. The first Tigard Public Library was opened on May 23, 1964, and was the inspiration of the Tigard Junior Women's Club in 1963, when they began planning. The first library was located at 12420 Southwest Main Street, moved to 12568 Southwest Main Street, and in 1986 it moved to the Tigard Civic Center at 13125 Southwest Hall Boulevard. Originally run by volunteers, the library added part-time staff in 1964, when the budget for the library was $175.

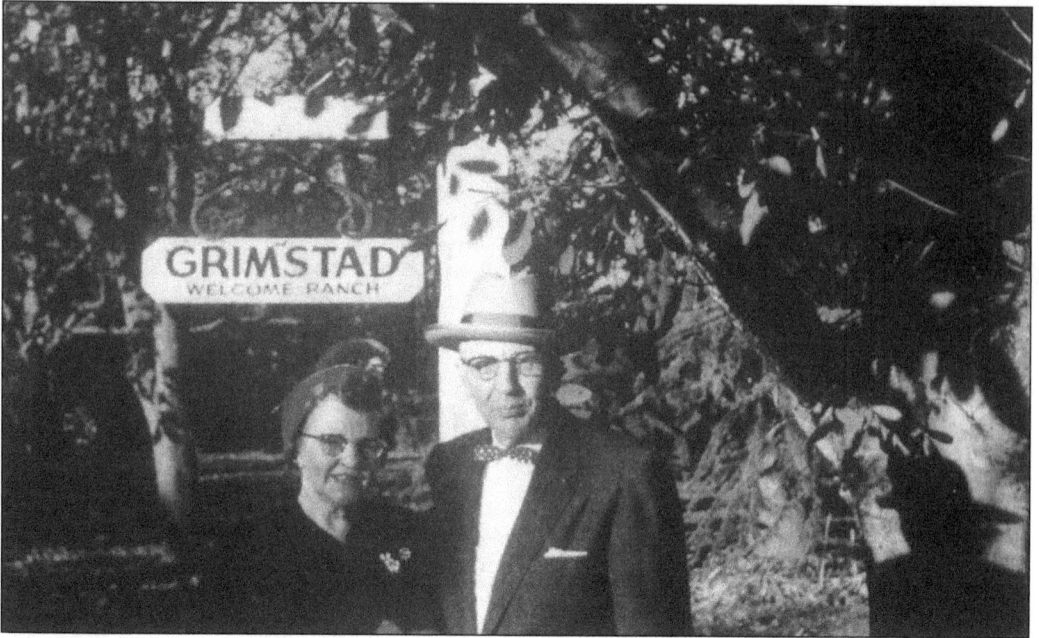

Joseph S. and Jennie Grimstad, pictured here, owned and operated Welcome Ranch on Highway 217, which later became Hall Boulevard from 1940 to 1963. The Grimstads' hobby was breeding and selling horses, such as Tennessee Walkers, and by 1947, raising Shetland ponies, for which they became famous. Their most endearing Shetland was "Toy Boy," a dappled chestnut pony. The Northwest Shetland Pony Club was organized on their ranch in June 1954. (Courtesy Paul Clark.)

Jennie Underland Grimstad, born in Bergen, Norway, wrote a children's book called *The Dappled Stallion*, based on her life experiences. Jennie and Joe Grimstad were parents to two children. In their retirement, the Grimstads moved from this five-room, white cottage at Welcome Ranch to King City in 1963. Welcome Ranch eventually became the location of the new Tigard Public Library. (Courtesy Paul Clark.)

20th ANNIVERSARY
Celebration

HOSTED BY THE BROADWAY ROSE THEATRE GUILD

Join us in honoring Broadway Rose founders Dan and Sharon and celebrating Broadway Rose's 20th Anniversary.

We will also be thanking those who have been with us through the years, including:

Collins Foundation
Harvey Platt
Susan Stark Haydon
Portland Spirit
Pearson Financial

WEDNESDAY, OCT. 5th, 2011

Light lunch and entertainment,
11:30 a.m. – 1 p.m.
at The New Stage, 12850 SW Grant Ave., Tigard

Tickets: $50 ($35 tax deductible)
Table of 10: $500 ($350 tax deductible)

Tigard Performing Arts Center was built in 1983 at a cost of $1.4 million. This auditorium for Tigard Senior High was financed by the Tigard School District. The Broadway Rose Theatre Company offers performances here during the summers. During the school year, student performances are presented to the public. The auditorium is named the Deb Fennell Auditorium to honor Tigard School District's former superintendent.

The Broadway Rose Theatre Company commemorated its 20th anniversary season with the world premier of the musical thriller *Ripper*. It was written by Duane Nelsen, directed by Abe Reybold, and included musical direction by Alan D. Lytle. A poster for *Ripper*, presented at the Deb Fennell Auditorium in August 2011, is pictured here. (Photograph by Craig Mitchelldyer; courtesy Broadway Rose Theatre Company and Craig Mitchelldyer.)

BROADWAY ROSE
THEATRE COMPANY
a world premiere musical thriller
Ripper
by Duane Nelsen

AUG. 3 - 21

TICKETS $20 - $35 • BOX OFFICE: 503.620.5262
Deb Fennell Auditorium, 9000 SW Durham Road, Tigard, OR 97223
OREGON'S PREMIER MUSICAL THEATRE COMPANY
WWW.BROADWAYROSE.ORG • GROUP RATES AVAILABLE

Tigard High School was built in 1953 on farmland formerly belonging to the Scheckla family. An active community academic center, it is the home of the Tigard Tigers. Next to the high school is the Tigard Swim Center. (Courtesy M.O. Stevens.)

The athletic stadium at Tigard High School was built with $300,000 in donations raised by the Tiger Pride Committee, volunteer boosters headed by Robert Gray, who built the stadium. Today, it is named the Robert A. Gray Stadium. This 2,000-seat, covered stadium offers a site for school and amateur sports, Easter services, special exhibitions, and concerts. It is the Tigard community center from which to watch Fourth of July Fireworks each year.

Cook Park is Tigard's largest, composed of 57 acres along the Tualatin River. It offers public picnic sites and fields for soccer, baseball, and football. The park is named for John Cook, who served as Tigard Park board chairman and was also mayor of Tigard from May 1984 through December 1986. Parks are developed in Tigard in keeping with the community development code and the economic development committee.

The Tualatin River runs through Cook Park and attracts canoe enthusiasts and kayakers. Tigard is a "green community," and is focused on health. The Tualatin River was an early freshwater attraction for the local region's Native Americans, the Atfalati Kalapuya, in addition to forming wetlands harboring wildlife and birds.

William Shaver was the son of Adam Shaver, an Oregon pioneer who had settled on a donation land claim in the area that became Tigard in 1852. William Shaver built his home in 1906, and today it is called the Quello House. Adam Shaver donated the land for the first Durham School on Durham Road.

Summerfield Golf and Country Club was constructed as an adult living community in Tigard between 1973 and 1980. This vast project was built by Summerfield's founder, Ron Sorensen (died 1978), who owned the Tualatin Development Corporation. He had built an earlier development for adults in retirement at King City in 1964.

The Tigard Balloon Festival is held annually during the month of June in Cook Park. Balloon clubs, businesses, private individuals, and radio stations sponsor balloons, which compete in a race for prizes. The Tigard Festival can be seen at tigardballoon.org and at Festival of Balloons, Tigard, Oregon. The festival is highlighted by the moon glow lighting of the balloons on Friday and Saturday evenings. Local nonprofit charities are assisted by this event. Ballooning is an intricate experience, with special care taken to fill each balloon with hot air generated by a propane burner system. Balloon layout on the ground is important; ropes and lines have to be untangled, and an extensive crew is necessary to fill and launch a balloon. A balloon flight begins with properly balancing the basket, or gondola, for carrying four to six passengers. (Photograph by the author.)

The historic John Tigard House, now a museum, is open to the public at least four times each year. The John Tigard House was built in 1880 on a Donation Land Claim signed by President Grant in 1873. The house was moved in 1979 from its original site on Pacific Highway facing McDonald Street to its present location at 103rd Street and Canterbury Lane. The museum is owned by the Tigard Historical Association and sits on leased city land. (Courtesy M.O. Stevens.)

Tigard's municipal civic center, approved by voters, was built in 1984. It contains the city's administrative offices, planning department, building department, finance, parks and recreation, police department, and originally, the Tigard Public Library. It was built for $2.2 million.

Tigard's Public Works Building, across from the civic center, houses Tigard's significant maintenance offices and displays a "Welcome to Downtown Tigard" sign. Tigard successfully combined rural values with metropolitan attractions and amenities. Hard work, integrity, and neighborliness are historical values that remain today.

These street scenes show modern-day downtown Tigard. Main Street is still the heart of the city. (Both, courtesy M.O. Stevens.)

The Tigard-Tualatin School District is 23J and includes Tigard High School (shown here about 1954 and built on former farmland), Tualatin High, Fowler Middle School, Hazelbrook Middle School, Twality Middle School, Bridgeport Elementary, Byrom Elementary, Charles F. Tigard Elementary, Durham Elementary, Mary Woodward Elementary, Metzger Elementary, Phil Lewis Elementary, Templeton Elementary, Tualatin Elementary, and Alberta Rider Elementary.

Tigard's newest elementary school, Alberta Rider Elementary, was built on land where Alberta and her husband, Charles Warren "Ren" Rider, had once lived in this log cabin on 20 acres of land. Alberta sold 7.3 acres to the Tigard-Tualatin School District, and the school was named for Alberta, called "a lifelong learner" and "champion of children." This 1870s cabin is typical of those of early Tigard pioneers.

Washington Square is the largest shopping center in Tigard, Oregon, located along Route 217. Its grand opening was held in February 1974 on 130 acres with over 100 stores and over a million square feet. It is one of the top-grossing malls in the United States and is currently owned by The Macerich Company. Tigard was awarded the right to annex this formerly unincorporated area in 1986. It is dominated by the 12-story Lincoln Center Tower. (Courtesy M.O. Stevens.)

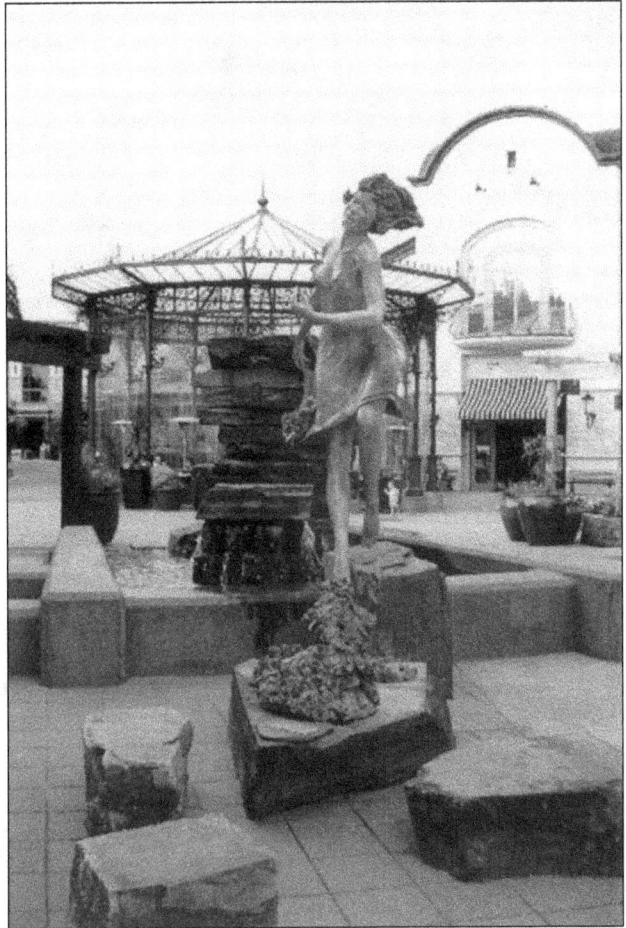

Bridgeport Village shopping center, opened in May 2005, is Tigard's most recent retail development. Currently operated by CenterCal Properties, it is a vital community gathering place, offering an 18-screen theatre, restaurants, and 90 stores. It is located between Tigard, Tualatin, Durham, and Lake Oswego, just west of Interstate 5 on a former Washington County-owned rock quarry. In 2006, the architect won a design and development award. Pictured below is a directory and listing of shops.

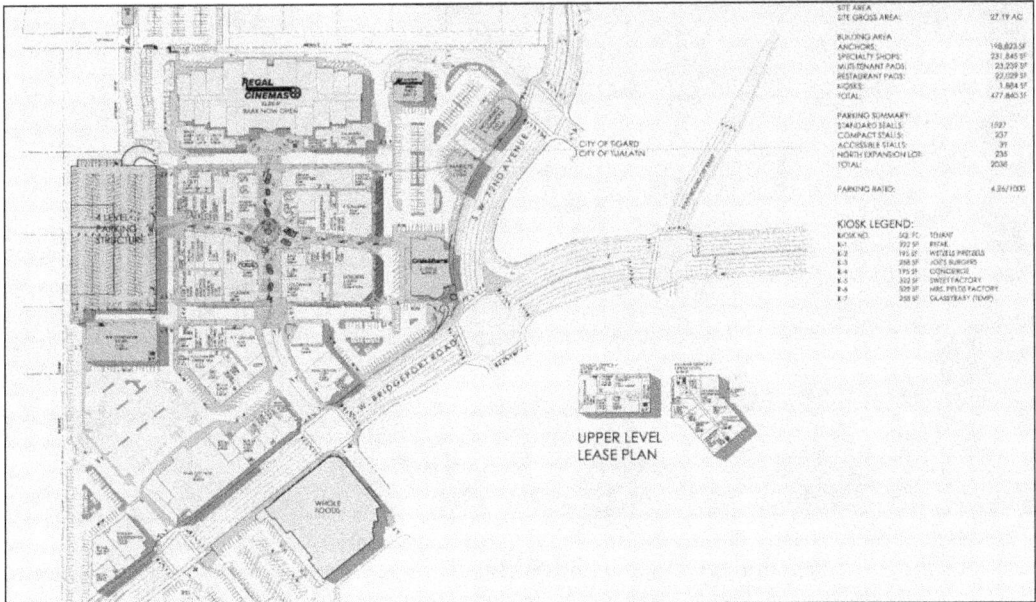

This plaque in Cook Park commemorates all Tigard "Centenarians." It was contributed by the City of Tigard and is maintained by the Girl Scouts Ti-Tu-Me-Wood Chapter and their friends. No. 12 on the list is Rosa Tigard.

BIBLIOGRAPHY

Carey, Charles Henry. *History of Oregon*. Vol. III, Portland, OR: The Pioneer Historical Publishing Co., 1922.

Corning, Howard McKinley. *Dictionary of Oregon History*. Portland, OR: Binfords and Mort, 1956.

Gaston, Joseph. *Portland, Oregon: Its History and Builders*. Portland, OR: S.J. Clarke Publishing Co., 1911.

Gaston, Joseph. The *Centennial History of Oregon 1811–1912*. Volumes I and II, Chicago: S.J. Clarke Publishing Company, 1912.

Genealogical Material in Oregon Donation Land Claims. Vol. I Genealogical Forum of Portland, Oregon Vol. I 1957, Vol. II 1959, Vol. III 1959, Vol. IV 1967, & Vol. V 1975.

Hagen, Robert D. *Totally Oregon*. Salem: Oregon Pride Productions, 1989.

Hines, H.K. *Illustrated History of the State of Oregon*. Chicago: Lewis Publishing Company, 1893.

Juntunen, Judy Rycroft, May D. Dasch, and Ann Bennett Rogers. The *World of the Kalapuya*. Philomath, OR: Benton County Historical Society and Museum, 2005.

Thomas C. Metsker. *Metsker's Atlas of Washington County Oregon*. Tacoma, WA. Located in Tigard Public Library's Local History Room 912.795 ref.

Payne, Mary. *Tigardville/Tigard: A History of Tigard*. Lake Oswego, OR: Lake Grove Printing Co., 1979, second edition. 1982.

Peterson, Barbara Bennett. *Peopling of the Americas, Currents, Canoes, and DNA*. New York: Nova Science Publishers, 2011.

Peterson, Barbara Bennett. *Summerfield History*. Tigard, OR: Summerfield Civic Association, 2011.

Records of Washington County Marriage Records, 1842–1880. Vol. I. Compiled by May Ringle Lepschat and Gyneth S. Balfour. Genealogical Forum of Portland, Oregon, 1972.

Records of Washington County Marriage Records, 1881–1896. Vol. II. Compiled by Gyneth S. Balfour. Genealogical Forum of Portland, Oregon, 1975.

Thompson, Richard. *Images of Rail: Willamette Valley Railways*. Charleston, SC: Arcadia Publishing, 2008.

INDEX

Visit us at
arcadiapublishing.com